APERTURE MASTERS OF PHOTOGRAPHY

APERTURE MASTERS OF PHOTOGRAPHY

TINA MODOTTI

KÖNEMANN

Frontispiece/Frontispiz/Frontispice: *Woman with flag,* 1928

Photographs courtesy:
front cover and frontispiece Throckmorton Fine Art, NY; p. 11 Margaret Hooks; pp. 13–17 Throckmorton Fine Art, NY;
p. 19 George Eastman House, Rochester, NY; p. 21 Throckmorton Fine Art, NY; p. 23 Philadelphia Museum of Art:
Gift of Mr. and Mrs. Carl Zigrosser; p. 25 The J. Paul Getty Museum, Los Angeles, CA; p. 27 National Gallery of Canada, Ottawa;
p. 29 The Minneapolis Institute of Arts, MN; pp. 31–37 Throckmorton Fine Art, NY; p. 39 Margaret Hooks;
p. 41 Center for Creative Photography, The University of Arizona, Tucson; p. 43 Margaret Hooks; p. 45 The Baltimore Museum of Art, MD:
Purchase with exchange funds from the Edward Joseph Gallagher III Memorial Collection, and Partial Gift of George H. Dalsheimer;
p. 47 Throckmorton Fine Art, NY; p. 49 The Art Institute of Chicago; p. 51 Fototeca del INAH, Mexico: Donation Carlos Vidali;
p. 53 Throckmorton Fine Art, NY; p. 55 collection National Gallery of Australia, Canberra; pp. 57–59 Throckmorton Fine Art, NY;
p. 61 Fototeca del INAH, Mexico: Donation Carlos Vidali; p. 63 Throckmorton Fine Art, NY; p. 65 Margaret Hooks;
p. 67 Throckmorton Fine Art, NY; p. 69 Cincinnati Art Museum, OH, Museum Purchase: Gift of the Estate of Clara J. Schawe,
Mrs. Ralph Robertson, and Lane Seminary, by exchange; p. 71 Throckmorton Fine Art, NY and Collection of Edmundo Kronfle, Jr.;
p. 73 Throckmorton Fine Art, NY; p. 75 Amon Carter Museum, Fort Worth, TX; p. 77 The Museum of Modern Art, NY,
courtesy of Isabel Carbajal Bolandi; p. 79 Throckmorton Fine Art, NY; p. 81 Fototeca del INAH, Mexico: Donation Carlos Vidali;
p. 83 Throckmorton Fine Art, NY; p. 85 Fototeca del INAH, Mexico: Donation Carlos Vidali; p. 87 The Bertram D. Wolfe Collection,
Hoover Institution Archives, Stanford, CA; pp. 89–91 Throckmorton Fine Art, NY; p. 92 New Orleans Museum of Art, LA;
back cover Throckmorton Fine Art, NY.

This 1999 edition is a coproduction from
Könemann Verlags GmbH, Bonner Str. 126, D–50968 Köln
and Aperture Foundation, Inc.
Subscribe to *Aperture*, the Quarterly, for just $50 U.S. for one year
or $86 U.S. for two years and you'll also receive a FREE copy of
Edward Weston: The Flame of Recognition with your paid subscription.
Write or email now to reserve your free book, a $27.50 value.
APERTURE 20 East 23rd Street, Dept. 447 New York, NY 10010.
Email: Circulation@Aperture.org. Or fax credit card orders to (212) 475-8790.

Coordination: Sally Bald and Susanne Kassung
Assistant: Monika Dauer
German translation: Andrea Hamann
French translation: Joëlle Marelli
Typesetting: Agentur Roman, Bold & Black
Cover design: Peter Feierabend
Production director: Detlev Schaper
Printing and binding: Sing Cheong Printing Co. Ltd., Hong Kong
Printed in Hong Kong, China

ISBN 3-8290-2888-1
10 9 8 7 6 5 4 3 2 1

TINA MODOTTI

Margaret Hooks

Now recognized as a seminal pre-war photographer, Tina Modotti (1896–1942) lived her life on the crest of the major movements in art and politics of the first half of the twentieth century. A thoroughly modern woman who smoked a pipe and was among the first to wear denim overalls, Modotti flouted convention in her personal and professional relationships, and in her photographs. As an engaged artist, she agonized over the conflict between life and art – between the purity of inspired creation and the demands of a world fractured by social injustice.

Modotti was familiar with social inequities from an early age. Born in the northern Italian city of Udine, one of her earliest memories was of her father, Giuseppe Modotti, lifting her high on his shoulders at a May Day rally to hear his fellow workers' songs and speeches. A few years later, in

Tina Modotti (1896–1942), die heute als eine der bedeutendsten Fotografinnen der Vorkriegsära gilt, lebte in einer Zeit, in der die bedeutenden künstlerischen und politischen Bewegungen der ersten Hälfte des 20. Jahrhunderts ihren Höhepunkt erreichten. Sie war eine moderne Frau, die Pfeife rauchte, als eine der ersten Drillichmonturen trug und sich in ihren privaten und beruflichen Beziehungen wie auch in ihrer fotografischen Arbeit über Konventionen hinwegsetzte. Als engagierte Künstlerin rang Modotti mit dem Widerspruch zwischen Leben und Kunst – zwischen der Reinheit kreativer Inspiration und den Anforderungen einer durch soziale Ungerechtigkeit geteilten Welt.

Modotti, die in der norditalienischen Stadt Udine geboren wurde, hatte von Kindesbeinen an soziale Ungerechtigkeit erlebt. In einer ihrer frühesten Erinnerungen hob ihr Vater, Giuseppe Modotti, sie bei einer Maikundgebung auf seine Schultern, damit sie die Lieder und Reden seiner Genossen hören

Aujourd'hui reconnue comme une photographe capitale de l'avant-guerre, Tina Modotti (1896–1942) passa sa vie à la pointe des mouvements les plus avancés en art et en politique dans la première moitié du XXᵉ siècle. Femme profondément moderne, fumant la pipe et parmi l'une des premières à porter des salopettes en jean, Modotti se moquait des conventions, dans ses relations personnelles ou professionnelles, comme dans son travail de photographe. Artiste engagée, elle souffrit toujours du conflit entre la vie et l'art – entre la pureté de la création inspirée et les exigences d'un monde divisé par l'injustice sociale.

Modotti avait été familiarisée avec les inégalités sociales dès son plus jeune âge. Née dans la ville d'Udine, dans le nord de l'Italie, l'un de ses plus anciens souvenir était son père, Giuseppe Modotti, la promenant sur ses épaules un 1ᵉʳ mai, pour aller entendre les chants et les discours politiques de ses

search of a better life for himself and his family, he emigrated to America. His departure plunged the family into a poverty that Tina would never forget. At barely fourteen years old, she became the family's only wage earner, working long, difficult hours in a local silk factory.

Over time, as his economic situation improved, Giuseppe sent for his wife and children to join him in San Francisco. Tina arrived in 1913 and quickly found a job as a seamstress in the prestigious I. Magnin department store. She was not long in the sewing room, however, before her romantic good looks attracted the attention of her employers, who hired her to model the store's latest fashions.

In 1915, San Francisco hosted the Pan-Pacific Exposition and there Tina first came into contact with modern art and photography movements. In its exotic ambience she also met and fell in love with her future husband, the soulful, bohemian painter and poet, Roubaix de l'Abrie Richey, known as Robo. Just one year later, she had given up modeling for acting in the local Italian theater, appearing mainly in some rather bad operettas. Nevertheless, Modotti's considerable acting talent and adoring public made her the toast of the neighborhood and probably led to her

konnte. Einige Jahre später emigrierte er in der Hoffnung auf ein besseres Leben für sich und seine Familie nach Amerika. Sein Weggang stürzte die Familie in tiefe Armut, die Tina Modotti nie vergessen sollte. Mit knapp 14 Jahren mußte sie den Lebensunterhalt für ihre Familie verdienen und den langen, anstrengenden Arbeitstag in einer örtlichen Seidenfabrik bewältigen.

Als es Giuseppe Modotti finanziell besser ging, ließ er Frau und Kinder nach San Francisco nachkommen. Tina traf 1913 ein und fand schnell eine Stellung als Näherin in dem renommierten Kaufhaus I. Magnin. Sie arbeitete noch nicht lange in der Nähstube, als ihren Arbeitgebern ihre romantisch anmutende Schönheit auffiel und sie sie engagierten, als Mannequin die neueste Mode des Hauses vorzuführen.

1915 richtete San Francisco die Pan-Pacific Exposition aus, bei der Tina erstmals mit den Strömungen der modernen Kunst und Fotografie in Berührung kam. In der exotischen Atmosphäre der Ausstellung lernte sie auch ihren späteren Ehemann kennen, den gefühlvollen, unkonventionellen Maler und Dichter Roubaix de l'Abrie Richey, genannt Robo. Ein Jahr später gab sie ihre Auftritte als Mannequin zugunsten der Schauspielerei am hiesigen italienischen Theater auf. Obgleich sie dort hauptsächlich in drittklassigen Operetten zu sehen war, wurde sie

camarades ouvriers. Quelques années plus tard, cherchant à améliorer ses conditions de vie et celles de sa famille, il émigra en Amérique. Son départ plongea la famille dans une pauvreté que Tina ne devait jamais oublier. A 14 ans à peine, elle devint la seule pourvoyeuse de revenus de la famille, travaillant de longues et pénibles heures dans une usine locale de soie.

Quelque temps après, comme sa situation s'améliorait, Giuseppe fit venir sa femme et ses enfants à San Francisco. Tina débarqua en 1913 et trouva rapidement un emploi comme couturière dans le prestigieux grand magasin I. Magnin. Il fallut peu de temps à ses employeurs pour remarquer sa beauté romanesque et pour l'engager comme mannequin présentant les dernières collections du magasin.

En 1915, San Francisco accueillit l'Exposition Pan-pacifique. C'est là que Tina fut pour la première fois confrontée aux l'art moderne et de la photographie. Dans cette atmosphère exotique, elle fit la connaissance et s'éprit de celui qui allait être son futur époux, Roubaix de l'Abrie Richey, peintre à la fois sensible et bohème, plus connu sous le nom de Robo. Un an plus tard, elle abandonnait la carrière de mannequin pour jouer dans le théâtre italien local, participant essentiellement à des opérettes de qualité médiocre. Malgré tout, son talent d'actrice et l'adoration de son public en

"discovery" by a talent scout from the growing silent film industry in Hollywood.

Tina Modotti arrived in Los Angeles in late 1918, and was cast in leading roles in the feature-length melodramas *The Tiger's Coat* and *I Can Explain*. However, she soon realized that Hollywood directors had difficulty imagining an Italian woman as anything other than a vamp. But there was more to Los Angeles than Hollywood for Modotti and Robo. They had become part of an avant-garde circle which included artists and anarchists, World War I draft evaders and dancers fascinated with art and free love, Eastern mysticism and the Mexican Revolution.

Through this new group of friends, Modotti met the well-known American photographer Edward Weston, then married with four young sons. In a letter to his close friend and fellow photographer Johan Hagemeyer, Weston wrote, "I not only have done some of the best things yet but also have had an exquisite affair... the pictures I believe to be particularly good are of one Tina de Richey – a lovely Italian girl."

wegen ihres beachtlichen schauspielerischen Talents und ihres hingebungsvollen Publikums zum gefeierten Star des Viertels und dadurch wahrscheinlich von einem Talentsucher der rasch wachsenden Stummfilmindustrie Hollywoods »entdeckt«.

Tina Modotti ging Ende 1918 nach Los Angeles und erhielt Hauptrollen in den melodramatischen Spielfilmen *The Tiger's Coat* und *I Can Explain*. Sie mußte allerdings schon bald feststellen, daß sich Hollywoods Regisseure eine italienische Frau eigentlich nur in der Rolle des Vamps vorstellen konnten. Los Angeles hatte Modotti und Robo jedoch mehr zu bieten als nur Hollywood. Sie gehörten einem avantgardistischen Zirkel an, der Künstler und Anarchisten, junge Männer, die im Ersten Weltkrieg dem Militärdienst entgangen waren, und Tänzer einschloß, die von Kunst und freier Liebe, östlichem Mystizismus und der mexikanischen Revolution fasziniert waren.

Durch diesen neuen Freundeskreis lernte Modotti den berühmten amerikanischen Fotografen Edward Weston kennen, der zu jenem Zeitpunkt noch verheiratet war und vier kleine Söhne hatte. In einem Brief an seinen engen Freund und Fotografenkollegen Johan Hagemeyer schrieb Weston: »Ich habe nicht nur einige meiner besten Aufnahmen gemacht, sondern auch eine wunderbare Affäre gehabt ... die Bilder, die

firent la coqueluche du quartier et furent sans doute à l'origine de sa « découverte » par un chasseur de talents de l'industrie hollywoodienne du film muet en pleine évolution.

Tina Modotti arriva à Los Angeles fin 1918 et obtint les rôles principaux de deux longs-métrages mélodramatiques, *The Tiger's Coat* et *I Can Explain*. Cependant, elle comprit vite que les réalisateurs de Hollywood ne pouvaient imaginer une Italienne dans le rôle d'une « vamp ». Mais aux yeux de Modotti et de Robo, Los Angeles était loin de se limiter à Hollywood. Ils faisaient partie d'un cercle d'avant-garde qui comprenait des artistes, des anarchistes, des jeunes hommes qui ont échappé aux obligations militaires lors de la première guerre mondiale, des danseurs, tous fascinés par l'art et l'amour libre, le mysticisme oriental et la révolution mexicaine.

C'est grâce à ce nouveau groupe d'amis que Modotti rencontra le célèbre photographe américain Edward Weston, alors marié et père de quatre garçons. Dans une lettre à son ami et collègue Johan Hagemeyer, Weston écrivit : « Non seulement j'ai fait les meilleures choses depuis longtemps, mais j'ai aussi eu une aventure délicieuse ... Les photos qui me paraissent particulièrement réussies sont d'une certaine Tina de Richey – une

Modotti viewed these striking portraits as a joint effort between artist and model, and this collaboration initiated one of the most exciting partnerships in photographic history.

Modotti and Weston's ongoing affair led Robo to remove himself temporarily to Mexico, where he died suddenly and tragically from smallpox just two days after Modotti had arrived to visit him. She stayed on in Mexico City to oversee an exhibit of his work and that of Edward Weston and other American photographers, but her stay was cut short by her father's sudden illness and subsequent death just a few weeks later.

This double loss and the deepening relationship with Weston brought about a new self-awareness in Modotti. She was no longer satisfied with the stereotypical parts she was being offered by Hollywood, nor with her role as model for the cameras of Edward Weston, Johan Hagemeyer, Jane Reece, and other members of Weston's circle. She began to run Weston's studio on occasion, go on photographic outings with him and Hagemeyer, and assist them in the

ich für besonders gut halte, sind von einer gewissen Tina de Richey – einer zauberhaften jungen Italienerin.« Modotti betrachtete diese bemerkenswerten Porträts als eine gemeinsame Leistung von Künstler und Modell. Mit ihrer Zusammenarbeit nahm eine der interessantesten Partnerschaften in der Geschichte der Fotografie ihren Anfang.

Modottis andauerndes Verhältnis mit Weston veranlaßte Robo, sich für einige Zeit nach Mexiko zurückzuziehen, wo er – zwei Tage, nachdem Modotti bei ihm zu Besuch war – unerwartet und tragisch einer Pockenerkrankung erlag. Sie entschloß sich, noch eine Weile in Mexico City zu bleiben, um eine Ausstellung mit Arbeiten von Robo, Edward Weston und anderen amerikanischen Fotografen zu organisieren. Ihr Aufenthalt fand jedoch ein jähes Ende, als ihr Vater plötzlich schwer erkrankte und wenige Wochen später starb.

Durch diesen zweifachen Verlust und die zunehmend intensive Beziehung zu Weston erlangte Modotti ein neues Selbstverständnis. Die stereotypen Rollen, die man ihr in Hollywood anbot, genügten ihr ebensowenig wie ihre Tätigkeit als Modell für die Fotografen Edward Weston, Johan Hagemeyer, Jane Reece und andere aus Westons Kreis. Sie begann, hin und wieder die Arbeit in Westons Atelier zu übernehmen, ihn und Hagemeyer bei Außenaufnahmen zu begleiten und ihnen in

jeune Italienne ravissante ». Ces étonnants portraits étaient considérés par Modotti comme le produit d'une collaboration entre l'artiste et le modèle, et ce fut le début de l'une des plus intéressantes associations dans l'histoire de la photographie.

La liaison entretenue par Modotti et Weston conduisit Robo à se retirer temporairement au Mexique où il mourut subitement et tragiquement de la variole, deux jours après que Modotti l'eût rejoint. Elle resta à Mexico pour superviser une exposition des travaux de Robo, de Weston et d'autres photographes américains, mais son séjour fut brutalement interrompu par la nouvelle de la maladie de son père et sa mort quelques semaines plus tard.

Cette double perte et la relation qui s'intensifiait entre elle et Weston suscitèrent une nouvelle prise de conscience chez Modotti. Elle ne pouvait plus se satisfaire des rôles stéréotypés que lui offrait Hollywood, ni de son rôle comme modèle devant les objectifs de Weston, de Johan Hagemeyer, de Jane Reece et des autres membres du cercle de Weston. Elle commença à travailler sporadiquement au studio de Weston, à l'accompagner ainsi que Hagemeyer au cours de leurs prises de vue en extérieur

darkroom. These experiences together with her childhood visits to the studio of her uncle, Pietro Modotti, a prominent Udine photographer, probably led to Modotti's later decision to establish her own photographic studio, a venture her father had also embarked on, albeit unsuccessfully, when he first arrived in San Francisco.

In July 1923, Modotti returned to Mexico, this time with Weston, his son Chandler, and an agreement that in exchange for helping him run his studio Weston would teach her photography. Post-revolutionary Mexico was in the throes of a social and cultural renaissance, and their Mexico City home became a renowned gathering place for artists, writers, and radicals such as Diego Rivera, Anita Brenner, and Jean Charlot. Their boisterous Saturday night parties were an opportunity for cross-dressing, plotting revolution, and exchanging ideas on art.

Under Weston's instruction Modotti developed rapidly as a photographer, and although his influence on her work is clear, she quickly took a direction of her own. Unafraid of experimentation, or of challenging Weston's purist max-

der Dunkelkammer zu assistieren. Diese Erfahrungen, wie auch ihre Kindheitserinnerungen an Besuche im Atelier ihres Onkels Pietro Modotti, der in Udine ein bekannter Fotograf war, haben Modotti sicherlich zur späteren Gründung eines eigenen Ateliers bewogen – ein Vorhaben, an dem sich auch ihr Vater in seiner Anfangszeit in San Francisco versucht hatte, allerdings ohne Erfolg.

Im Juli 1923 kehrte Modotti nach Mexiko zurück, diesmal mit Weston und dessen Sohn Chandler – und mit der Übereinkunft, daß Weston ihr als Gegenleistung für ihre Arbeit in seinem Atelier das Fotografieren beibringen würde. Im post-revolutionären Mexiko war gerade die gesellschaftliche und kulturelle Erneuerung in vollem Gange, und ihr Haus in Mexico City entwickelte sich zu einem bekannten Treffpunkt von Künstlern, Schriftstellern und Radikalen wie Diego Rivera, Anita Brenner und Jean Charlot. Ihre turbulenten samstäglichen Partys boten Gelegenheit, in die Kleider und Rolle des jeweils anderen Geschlechts zu schlüpfen, revolutionäre Pläne zu schmieden und Ansichten über Kunst zu diskutieren.

Unter Westons Anleitung machte Modotti als Fotografin rasche Fortschritte. Wenn sein Einfluß auf ihre Arbeiten auch unübersehbar ist, ging sie doch schon bald eigene Wege. Ohne jede Scheu, zu experimentieren und

et à les assister au développement. Ces expériences, alliées au souvenir de ses visites d'enfant dans l'atelier de son oncle, Pietro Modotti, photographe éminent à Udine, furent sans doute à l'origine de la décision de Modotti d'installer son propre studio, reprenant l'aventure que son père avait entreprise à son arrivée à San Francisco, mais qui avait été à l'époque un échec.

En juillet 1923, Modotti retourna au Mexique, cette fois avec Weston, son fils Chandler et un accord aux termes duquel Weston lui apprendrait la photographie en échange de son aide au studio. Le Mexique post-révolutionnaire était en pleine efferrescence sociale et culturelle et leur maison de Mexico devint un lieu de réunion célèbre où se retrouvaient artistes, écrivains et radicaux, tels que Diego Rivera, Anita Brenner ou Jean Charlot. Le samedi soir, des fêtes tumultueuses étaient l'occasion de se travestir, de fomenter des révolutions et d'échanger des idées sur l'art.

Instruite par Weston, Modotti acquit rapidement la maîtrise de la photographie et, bien que l'influence de ce dernier soit évidente, prit rapidement un chemin autonome. Ne craignant pas d'expérimenter, ni de remettre en ques-

ims, she cropped and enlarged many of her images and explored the potential of multiple exposures and photomontage. From Weston, Modotti learned the principles of modernist photography and made several images in this vein, such as *Roses, Telephone wires*, and *Doors*.

But the longer she was in Mexico the more she felt the need to respond through her photography to the upheavals over land reform and social injustice roiling the nation. This impulse led to some of her best work, a melding of a modernist aesthetic with Mexican revolutionary culture – she was able to take form and give it content. Examples of this are *Workers parade*, a shot of a column of peasant farmers marching on May Day 1926; *Mexican peasant boy*; and the carefully composed "icons" of the revolution – the sombrero, the bandolier, the guitar, and the ear of corn – in the series "Study for a Mexican Song."

At the center of Mexico's cultural revolution were the larger-than-life muralists who competed for wall space for their magnificent, gargantuan paintings. Through her friendship with these painters, especially Diego Rivera,

Westons puristische Maximen in Frage zu stellen, beschnitt oder vergrößerte sie viele ihrer Aufnahmen und erkundete die Möglichkeiten der Mehrfachbelichtung und der Fotomontage. Von Weston lernte Modotti die Grundlagen der modernistischen Fotografie, die sie in Aufnahmen wie *Roses, Telephone wires* und *Doors* umsetzte.

Je länger sie jedoch in Mexiko war, desto stärker verspürte sie die Notwendigkeit, mit ihrer Fotografie auf die Unruhen zu reagieren, die das Land aufgrund der Landreform und der sozialen Mißstände erschütterten. Aus diesem Bedürfnis heraus entstanden einige ihrer besten Arbeiten, in der sie eine Verbindung der modernistischen Ästhetik mit der revolutionären Kultur Mexikos herstellte – sie verstand es, die von ihr gewählte Form mit Inhalt zu füllen. Gute Beispiele dafür sind: *Workers parade*, ein Schnappschuß einer Kolonne von Landarbeitern anläßlich der Maifeier 1926, *Mexican peasant boy* und die mit Bedacht zusammengestellten »Ikonen« der Revolution – der Sombrero, der Patronengurt, die Gitarre und der Maiskolben – in der Serie »Study for a Mexican Song«.

Eine zentrale Rolle in der mexikanischen Kulturrevolution spielten die Wandmaler, die um Flächen für ihre imposanten, monumentalen Malereien konkurrierten. Durch ihre Freundschaft mit diesen Malern, insbesondere mit

tion le purisme de Weston, elle ne se privait pas de recadrer et d'agrandir ses images, explorant les potentialités de la surimpression et du photomontage. De Weston, Modotti apprit les principes du modernisme photographique et réalisa plusieurs images dans cette veine, comme *Roses, Telephone wires* et *Doors*.

Mais plus son séjour à Mexico se prolongeait, plus elle éprouvait la nécessité de réagir par le truchement de la photographie aux bouleversements liés à la réforme agraire et à l'injustice sociale qui agitaient le pays. Cette impulsion donna naissance à certaines de ses meilleures œuvres, où se fondent esthétique moderniste et culture révolutionnaire mexicaine, montrant son aptitude à utiliser un langage formel et à lui donner un contenu. Il en va ainsi dans *Workers parade*, où l'on voit une colonne de paysans défilant pour le 1er mai 1926, dans *Mexican peasant boy* et dans les icônes soigneusement composées de la révolution – le sombrero, la cartouchière, la guitare, l'épi de maïs, dans la série intitulée « Study for a Mexican Song ».

Au cœur de la révolution culturelle mexicaine se trouvaient les fresquistes monumentaux toujours en concurrence pour trouver un espace mural apte à recevoir leurs somptueuses et immenses peintures. Son amitié avec ces peintres,

for whom she posed on several occasions, Modotti became the most sought-after photographer of their work. As a result of this close working relationship, she became influenced by the muralists' communist ideas and ideals. But Modotti was not a political theorist and was seemingly naive about the ideological debates taking place among Communists at the time. Her political involvement at this point was primarily to participate in campaigns to free political prisoners and to help promote international liberation movements. Not surprisingly, Modotti was experiencing difficulty in fusing the many facets of her life. "Art cannot exist without life," she wrote at the time, "but... in my case life is always struggling to predominate and art naturally suffers."

Her growing social conscience was driving her and Weston apart and she had put their relationship on a platonic footing. Moreover, he missed his children and wanted to return to the United States, while she wanted to stay in Mexico, where she not only felt at home in the midst of the social upheaval but felt she had a role in it. Their separation in November 1926 marked an end to their Mexican idyll. It saddened both, and though they

Diego Rivera, für den sie mehrfach Modell stand, wurde Modotti zur gefragtesten Fotografin für die Arbeiten dieser Künstler. Im Laufe dieser intensiven Arbeitsbeziehung wurde sie von kommunistischen Ideen und Idealen der Wandmaler beeinflußt. Modotti war jedoch keine politische Theoretikerin und wußte anscheinend wenig über die ideologischen Auseinandersetzungen, die die Kommunisten jener Zeit führten. Ihr politisches Engagement bestand zu diesem Zeitpunkt hauptsächlich darin, an Kampagnen zur Freilassung politischer Gefangener mitzuwirken und internationale Befreiungsbewegungen zu unterstützen. Es ist kaum verwunderlich, daß sie mitunter Schwierigkeiten hatte, die zahlreichen Facetten ihres Lebens in Einklang zu bringen. »Die Kunst kann ohne das Leben nicht existieren«, schrieb Modotti damals, »aber... in meinem Fall versucht das Leben immer, die Oberhand zu gewinnen, und darunter leidet natürlich die Kunst.«

Ihr wachsendes soziales Bewußtsein führte dazu, daß sie und Weston sich auseinanderlebten und sie ihre Beziehung fortan als eine rein platonische Freundschaft betrachtete. Hinzu kam, daß er seine Kinder vermißte und es ihn in die Vereinigten Staaten zurück zog, während Modotti in Mexiko bleiben wollte, wo sie sich inmitten des gesellschaftlichen Umbruchs nicht nur wohl fühlte, sondern auch das Gefühl hatte, ihren Beitrag leisten zu müssen. Ihre

en particulier avec Diego Rivera pour qui elle posa à maintes reprises, fit de Modotti la photographe la plus recherchée pour ce type de travaux. Le résultat de ce travail en étroite collaboration fut l'influence qu'exercèrent sur elle les idées et les idéaux communistes des fresquistes. Mais Modotti n'était pas une théoricienne de la politique et était peu impliquée dans les débats idéologiques entre communistes à cette époque. Son engagement politique pendant cette période consistait à participer aux campagnes de libération des prisonniers politiques et à contribuer à promouvoir les mouvements de libération internationaux. Il n'est guère surprenant que Modotti éprouvât de la difficulté à concilier les différentes facettes de sa vie. « L'art ne peut exister sans la vie », écrivit-elle à la même époque, « mais... dans mon cas, la vie cherche toujours à prendre le dessus et naturellement l'art en souffre ».

L'acuité toujours plus grande de sa conscience sociale l'éloignait de Weston et elle en vint à donner à leur relation un tour platonique. En outre, il se languissait de ses enfants et voulait rentrer aux Etats-Unis, tandis qu'elle désirait rester à Mexico où non seulement elle se sentait chez elle au milieu des bouleversements sociaux mais avait aussi l'intuition qu'elle avait un rôle à y jouer. La rupture eut lieu en novembre 1926, marquant la fin de l'idylle mexicaine.

Jean Charlot, 1924

never saw each other again, they communicated frequently, sharing their work and innermost thoughts, until 1931, when Modotti's new life in Stalinist Russia led her to sever all communication with him.

Following Weston's departure, Modotti entered her most productive period as a photographer, running her own professional studio and creating some of her most commanding images: *Mella's typewriter*, *Hands resting on tool*, and *Worker carrying beam*. Her work can be divided loosely into four categories: photographs of Mexico and Mexican folk art for leading art periodicals and her documentation of the work of renowned Mexican artists for publication in books; photojournalism for *El Machete*, which includes the majority of her most poignant studies of the disparities in Mexican society, together with her documentation of Communist Party rallies, reunions, and other events; her studio "bread and butter" work – professional portraits of Mexico's rich, famous, and outrageous; and the images she made for pure pleasure – the sensual forms of slender lilies, the sinuous shapes of women embracing their children, and the strong abstract lines of wood scaffolding and telegraph wire.

Trennung im November 1926 bedeutete das Ende ihrer mexikanischen Idylle und erfüllte beide mit Traurigkeit. Auch wenn sie sich nie wiedersehen sollten, blieben sie doch in regem Kontakt und tauschten sich über ihre Arbeit und ihre intimsten Gedanken aus, bis Modotti 1931 im stalinistischen Rußland ein neues Leben begann und die Verbindung zu ihm abbrach.

Nach Westons Abreise begann Modottis produktivste Phase als Fotografin. Sie führte ihr eigenes professionelles Atelier und schuf einige ihrer eindrucksvollsten Aufnahmen: *Mella's typewriter*, *Hands resting on tool* und *Worker carrying beam*. Ihre Arbeiten lassen sich grob in vier Kategorien einteilen: Aufnahmen von Mexiko und der mexikanischen Volkskunst für führende Kunstzeitschriften sowie ihre Dokumentation über die Werke bekannter mexikanischer Künstler für Veröffentlichungen in Buchform; fotojournalistische Arbeiten für die Zeitschrift *El Machete*, darunter die Mehrzahl ihrer packenden Studien über soziale Gegensätze in der mexikanischen Gesellschaft sowie ihre Dokumentationen über Massenkundgebungen, Versammlungen und anderen Veranstaltungen der Kommunistischen Partei; ihre einträglichen Atelierarbeiten »fürs tägliche Brot« – professionelle Porträts der reichen und prominenten Oberschicht Mexikos; und schließlich die Aufnahmen, die sie zu ihrem reinen Vergnügen machte –

Tous deux en furent attristés et, bien qu'ils ne se revissent jamais, ils restèrent en contact permanent, partageant des réflexions sur leurs travaux et leurs pensées les plus intimes jusqu'en 1931, date à laquelle l'installation de Modotti dans la Russie de Staline interrompit toute communication entre eux.

Après le départ de Weston, Modotti entra dans sa période la plus productive en tant que photographe, installant son propre studio et réalisant certaines de ses images les plus marquantes : *Mella's typewriter*, *Hands resting on tool*, ou encore *Worker carrying beam*. Son œuvre peut être divisée grossièrement en quatre catégories : les photos de Mexico et de l'art populaire mexicain pour les grandes revues d'art, ainsi que les reproductions d'œuvres d'artistes mexicains célèbres destinés à paraître sous forme de livres ; les travaux de photojournalisme pour le journal *El Machete*, y compris la majorité de ses poignantes études sur les disparités de la société mexicaine, avec des images de manifestations et de rassemblements du Parti communiste ou d'autres événements politiques du même ordre ; ses travaux « alimentaires » faits en studio – portraits de commande des personnalités riches ou célèbres de Mexico ; enfin les images qu'elle faisait pour son propre plaisir – lys sensuels et élancés, formes sinueuses de femmes embrassant leurs enfants ou encore les

die sinnlichen Formen schmaler Lilien, die geschmeidigen Körper von Frauen, die ihre Kinder umarmen, und die markanten, abstrakten Linien von Holzgerüsten und Telegrafenleitungen.

lignes puissantes et abstraites des échafaudages en bois ou des fils télégraphiques.

Modotti's home had become a hive of activity for Latin American exiles as her support for their liberation struggles grew. It was also a gathering place for Mexican artists such as Rufino Tamayo, the photographer Manuel Álvarez Bravo, and the young Frida Kahlo. In 1928, she began living with the dynamic young Cuban revolutionary-in-exile, Julio Antonio Mella. They had been together only a few months when he was gunned down at her side on a dark Mexico City street by his political opponents.

In Modottis Haus trafen sich immer mehr im Exil lebende Lateinamerikaner, da sie die Befreiungsbewegungen in deren Ländern zunehmend unterstützte. Zudem war es ein Treffpunkt für mexikanische Künstler wie Rufino Tamayo, den Fotografen Manuel Álvarez Bravo und die junge Frida Kahlo. Ab 1928 lebte Modotti mit dem jungen Kubaner Julio Antonio Mella zusammen, einem dynamischen Revolutionär, der in Mexiko im Exil lebte. Sie kannten sich erst wenige Monate, als Mella in einer dunklen Gasse in Mexico City an Modottis Seite von politischen Gegnern erschossen wurde.

La demeure de Modotti était devenue un foyer d'activité pour les exilés d'Amérique latine dont elle soutenait activement les luttes de libérations nationales. C'était aussi un lieu de rendez-vous pour des artistes mexicains comme Rufino Tamayo, le photographe Manuel Álvarez Bravo et la jeune Frida Kahlo. En 1928, elle partageait depuis quelques mois la vie d'un jeune révolutionnaire cubain en exil, Julio Antonio Mella, lorsqu'il fut un jour abattu devant elle par des opposants politiques dans une sombre rue de Mexico.

Despite the murder's obvious political overtones, the Mexican government used the trial to attack the Communists, trying to show they were immoral by implicating Modotti in a "crime of passion." The ensuing investigation became a virtual inquisition on her sexuality. Her home was ransacked by the police and Weston's nude studies of her were seized as proof of her immorality, causing irreparable damage to her reputation and career. On the one hand, there was the embarrassment of the Communist Party rank and file, modest farmers and workers unfamiliar

Obgleich der Mord offensichtlich einen politischen Hintergrund hatte, benutzte die mexikanische Regierung den anschließenden Prozeß als Vorwand zu einem Feldzug gegen die Kommunisten. Sie versuchte, diese als sittenlos darzustellen, indem sie Modotti in einen »Mord aus Leidenschaft« verwickelte. Bei den nachfolgenden Ermittlungen wurde ihr Sexualleben einer regelrechten Inquisition unterzogen. Die Polizei durchwühlte Modottis Wohnung und beschlagnahmte Aktstudien, die Weston von ihr gemacht hatte, als Beweis für ihre Unmoral. Ihrem Ansehen und ihrer be-

En dépit du caractère clairement politique de cet assassinat, le gouvernement mexicain se servit du procès contre les communistes, essayant de démontrer leur supposée immoralité en impliquant Modotti dans un « crime passionnel ». L'enquête qui s'ensuivit prit la tournure d'une véritable inquisition sur sa vie sexuelle. Sa maison fut retournée par la police et les études de nus que Weston avait fait d'elle saisies comme preuve de son immoralité, ce qui causa un tort irréparable à sa réputation et à sa carrière. D'une part, il y avait l'embarras de la base du parti communiste, paysans et

Calla lily, ca. 1925

with art photography who did not understand the context of these works, and on the other, the horror of leading members of Mexican society, whose portraits Modotti earned her living making, reading in their daily newspapers that their nice Italian photographer was in fact a "depraved communist."

Eventually Modotti was acquitted, but Mella's assassination and the ordeal of the trial brought home to her the virulent reaction that could occur in the struggle to bring about social change. Although she emerged emotionally battered and mentally exhausted from the experience, it strengthened her and irrevocably changed her perception of the world. She no longer felt there was any middle ground; life for her was now a matter of absolutes. If previously she had been a photographer with a cause, she was now a revolutionary with a mission. A new zeal drove her to follow in Mella's footsteps.

And as a photographer, what better way to do so than to continue the work they had done for the Mexican

ruflichen Laufbahn wurden durch diese Schmutzkampagne irreparabler Schaden zugefügt. Auf der einen Seite war da die peinliche Betroffenheit der kommunistischen Parteibasis – einfache Bauern und Arbeiter, denen künstlerische Fotografie fremd war und die den Kontext dieser Werke nicht verstanden – und auf der anderen Seite das Entsetzen der mexikanischen Oberschicht, mit deren Porträts Modotti ihren Lebensunterhalt bestritt und die nun bei der täglichen Zeitungslektüre erfuhr, daß ihre nette italienische Fotografin in Wahrheit eine »verdorbene Kommunistin« war.

Schließlich wurde Modotti freigesprochen, aber die Ermordung Mellas und die Tortur des Prozesses hatten ihr klargemacht, welch scharfe Reaktionen der Kampf um gesellschaftliche Veränderungen hervorrufen konnte. Wenngleich sie dieses Erlebnis emotional niederschmetterte und geistig erschöpfte, ging sie aus den Erfahrungen doch gestärkt und mit einer veränderten Weltsicht hervor. Sie glaubte nicht mehr an einen Mittelweg. Für sie gab es jetzt nur noch absolute Antworten. War sie vorher eine Fotografin gewesen, die sich für eine Sache einsetzte, so war sie nun eine Revolutionärin mit einer Mission. Neuer Eifer trieb sie an, Mellas Beispiel zu folgen.

Für sie als Fotografin gab es wohl kaum eine bessere Möglichkeit, als ihre Arbeit für die Zeitung der mexikanischen

ouvriers peu familiarisés avec l'art photographique et qui ne comprenaient pas le contexte de ces travaux ; d'autre part, la répulsion des membres de la haute société mexicaine dont Modotti faisait les portraits pour gagner sa vie et qui lisaient dans leurs quotidiens que leur charmante photographe italienne était en réalité une « communiste dépravée ».

Modotti finit par être acquittée, mais l'assassinat de Mella et l'épreuve du procès provoquèrent chez elle une violente réaction qui trouva à s'exprimer dans la lutte pour le changement social. Elle en sortit émotionnellement meurtrie et mentalement épuisée, mais renforcée par l'expérience et avec une perception du monde irrévocablement changée. Il n'y avait plus pour elle de moyen terme ; la vie était désormais affaire d'absolus. Elle avait été une photographe engagée, elle était désormais une révolutionnaire pourvue d'une mission. Un zèle nouveau la poussait à suivre les traces de Mella.

En tant que photographe, quel meilleur moyen y avait-il d'y parvenir qu'en poursuivant le travail qu'ils avaient fait

Communist Party (PCM) newspaper *El Machete*? In 1928, when Mella was the paper's chief writer, Modotti had published an innovative series in the paper under the title, "The Contrasts of the Regime." Images of poverty and degradation such as *Misery* and *Poverty and elegance* were juxtaposed with images of wealth to reveal the discrepancies of post-revolutionary Mexico. Soon after Mella's death, on May Day 1929, Modotti took her photojournalism a step further with an assignment from *El Machete* to cover a march protesting the crackdown on the PCM. The eighteen images made that day with her Graflex camera depict the event's relaxed, jovial beginning, follow it through Mexico City's streets to the United States embassy, capture the subsequent arrival of the police to disperse the crowd, and record the violence of the march's end.

These images show that Modotti was at ease with reportage, moving quickly to record dramatic events. This new, more aggressive role indicates a change in attitude; the slow, careful composition and aesthetic of an image were no longer of such importance to her.

Kommunistischen Partei (PCM), *El Machete,* fortzuführen. 1928, als Mella Hauptautor der Zeitung war, hatte Modotti darin unter dem Titel »Die Gegensätze des Regimes« eine neuartige Fotoserie veröffentlicht. Aufnahmen von Armut und Verelendung, wie *Misery* und *Poverty and elegance,* wurden Bilder von Reichtum gegenübergestellt, um die Widersprüche der postrevolutionären mexikanischen Gesellschaft zu verdeutlichen. Bald nach Mellas Tod, am 1. Mai 1929, ging Modotti in ihrer fotojournalistischen Arbeit noch einen Schritt weiter: *El Machete* hatte sie beauftragt, über eine Protestdemonstration anläßlich der staatlichen Übergriffe auf die Kommunistische Partei zu berichten. Die 18 Aufnahmen, die sie an jenem Tag mit ihrer Graflex-Kamera machte, zeigen den fröhlichen Beginn der Veranstaltung, folgen ihr durch die Straßen von Mexico City zur amerikanischen Botschaft, dokumentieren das anschließende Eintreffen der Polizei mit dem Ziel, die Menge auseinanderzutreiben, und halten die Gewalttätigkeiten am Ende der Demonstration fest.

Diese Bilder zeigen, wie vertraut Modotti mit der Reportage war, wie beweglich und schnell sie bei der Dokumentation dramatischer Ereignisse reagierte. Diese neue, aggressivere Rolle läßt eine veränderte Einstellung erkennen; die langsame, sorgfältige Komposition und Ästhetik eines Bildes waren ihr nicht mehr so wichtig.

ensemble pour le journal du Parti communiste mexicain (PCM), *El Machete ?* En 1928, Mella était alors rédacteur en chef du journal. Modotti y avait publié une série de photos novatrices sous le titre « Les contrastes du régime ». Des images de pauvreté et de dégradation, intitulées *Misery* ou *Poverty and elegance,* étaient confrontées à des images de richesse afin de révéler les contradictions du Mexique post-révolutionnaire. Peu après la mort de Mella, le 1ᵉʳ mai 1929, Modotti poussait encore plus loin sa pratique du photojournalisme, en couvrant pour *El Machete* une manifestation contre les mesures de répression prises à l'encontre du PCM. Les 18 images prises ce jour là avec son appareil Graflex montrent le début jovial et détendu de la marche, que l'on suit le long des rues de Mexico jusqu'à l'ambassade des Etats-Unis, captant sur le vif l'arrivée de la police venue disperser la foule, et gardant la trace des violences qui mirent fin à la manifestation.

Ces images montrent que Modotti était à l'aise dans le reportage, se déplaçant rapidement pour enregistrer les événements importants. Ce rôle nouveau, plus offensif, indique un changement d'attitude ; la composition lente et attentive d'une image esthétique n'était plus son souci principal.

In an interview with Carleton Beals for a 1929 article on her photography in *Creative Art*, Modotti described her new outlook as a desire to produce nothing other than "the perfect snapshot." By snapshot she did not mean amateur, but rather, impromptu photographs. "The moving quality of life rather than still studies absorb her," Beals wrote.

Later that year, following a visit to the Isthmus of Tehuantepec, famed for its strong, strikingly handsome women, Modotti wrote to Weston that the photographs she had taken there were "snapshots." With some wonderful exceptions, many of the photographs made on that trip do have that quality, and appear to be largely an attempt to document the customs, environs, and apparel of the women of this region.

Back in Mexico City, scandal continued to follow Modotti, as did the secret police, who kept vigil outside her home. It further erupted when her first solo exhibition opened in December 1929. The "First Revolutionary Photography Exhibit" reflected Modotti's preoccupations with producing "revolutionary" art, indicative of which was

In einem Interview mit Carleton Beals für einen 1929 in der Zeitschrift *Creative Art* erschienenen Artikel über ihre Fotografie beschreibt Modotti ihren neuen Ansatz als den Wunsch, nichts anderes als »den perfekten Schnappschuß« zu produzieren. Dabei verstand sie unter einem Schnappschuß nicht etwa laienhafte, sondern improvisierte Aufnahmen. »Der Bewegungsaspekt des Lebens fasziniert sie mehr als Standstudien«, schrieb Beals.

Nach einer Reise, die Modotti im selben Jahr zum Isthmus von Tehuantepec führte – ein Landstrich, der für seine starken, auffallend schönen Frauen gerühmt wird –, bezeichnete sie ihre dort gemachten Aufnahmen in einem Brief an Weston als »Schnappschüsse«. Bis auf einige wundervolle Ausnahmen haben viele der auf dieser Reise entstandenen Fotos in der Tat den Charakter eines Schnappschusses und erwecken den Eindruck, als habe die Fotografin primär versucht, die Bräuche, den Lebensraum und die Trachten der Frauen dieser Region zu dokumentieren.

Zurück in Mexico City wurde Modotti nicht nur weiterhin von Skandalgeschichten verfolgt, sondern auch von der Geheimpolizei, die ihr Haus ständig überwachte. Die Situation spitzte sich zu, als im Dezember 1929 ihre erste Einzelausstellung eröffnet wurde. Die »Erste Ausstellung Revolutionärer Fotografie« spiegelte Modottis Anliegen

Dans une interview avec Carleton Beals destinée à un article de 1929 sur son travail dans *Creative Art,* Tina Modotti définissait son nouveau regard comme correspondant au désir de ne produire rien d'autre qu'un « instantané parfait ». Elle entendait par là, non pas l'idée d'une photographie d'amateur, mais celle d'une photographie impromptue. « Plutôt que l'étude figée, c'est la qualité de mouvement de la vie qui l'absorbe », écrivit Beals.

Quelques mois plus tard, après un voyage dans l'isthme de Tehuantepec, dont les femmes étaient célèbres pour leur force et leur saisissante beauté, Modotti écrivit à Weston que les photos qu'elle y avait faites étaient des « instantanés ». A quelques remarquables exceptions près, de nombreuses images de ce voyage ont, en effet, cette qualité et apparaissent comme une tentative de témoigner des coutumes, de l'habillement et du cadre de vie des femmes de cette région.

De retour à Mexico, Modotti était toujours poursuivie par le scandale, ainsi que par la police secrète qui postait en permanence des vigiles devant sa porte. Un nouveau rebondissement eut lieu lors de sa première exposition personnelle, en décembre 1929. La « Première exposition de photographie révolutionnaire » reflétait la volonté de produire un

Mother and child, Tehuantepec, 1929

her choice of the firebrand muralist David Alfaro Siqueiros to inaugurate the show. He was arrested a few days later for conspiring against the government and in the ensuing publicity, Modotti's lifestyle was once again dragged into the Mexican press. Ironically, in the midst of this political activity, Modotti's photography was gaining more international recognition; articles on her work were appearing in magazines such as *Creative Art*, *transition*, and *BIFUR*, and Agfa was using her endorsement to sell their film.

In early 1930, an attempt on the Mexican president's life and a subsequent crackdown on PCM members led to Modotti's arrest and deportation to Europe. On the boat to Europe, she deepened her friendship with Soviet agent Vittorio Vidali, a fellow Italian she had met in Mexico in 1927. He tried to persuade her to accompany him to Moscow, but she wanted to go to Berlin. While there, she came into contact with the Bauhaus school of photographers and designers, with whose work she was already familiar through publications she had seen in Mexico. She met local photographer Lotte Jacobi, who organized an exhibit of Modotti's work, which was well received by local critics. But Modotti found it impossible to adjust to her

wider, »revolutionäre« Kunst zu schaffen, was sich auch darin äußerte, daß auf ihren Wunsch der aufrührerische Wandmaler David Alfaro Siqueiros die Eröffnungsrede hielt. Wenige Tage später wurde er wegen verschwörerischer Aktivitäten gegen die Regierung verhaftet, und in der nachfolgenden Berichterstattung fiel die mexikanische Presse erneut über Modottis Lebensstil her. Merkwürdigerweise fand Modottis Fotografie ausgerechnet in dieser politisch aktiven Phase größere internationale Anerkennung. In Zeitschriften wie *Creative Art, transition* und *BIFUR* erschienen Artikel über ihre Arbeit, und Agfa warb mit ihr für seine Filme.

Ein Anschlag auf den mexikanischen Präsidenten zu Beginn des Jahres 1930 und das anschließend harte Vorgehen der Staatsmacht gegen die Mitglieder der Kommunistischen Partei führten zu Modottis Verhaftung und Abschiebung nach Europa. Bei der Überfahrt auf dem Schiff traf sie den sowjetischen Agenten Vittorio Vidali, einen Landsmann, den sie 1927 in Mexiko kennengelernt hatte, und vertiefte ihre Freundschaft mit ihm. Er versuchte, sie zu überreden, mit ihm nach Moskau zu kommen, sie zog es jedoch nach Berlin. Während ihrer Zeit dort knüpfte sie Kontakte mit den Fotografen und Designern des Bauhaus, deren Werke sie bereits durch Publikationen aus ihrer Zeit in Mexiko kannte. Die Fotografin Lotte Jacobi organisierte eine Ausstel-

art qui fût « révolutionnaire ». Cela se reflète dans le choix que porta Modotti sur David Alfaro, peintre provocateur, pour faire le discours d'inauguration. Le fresquiste fut arrêté quelques jours plus tard pour conspiration contre le gouvernement. La publicité qui s'ensuivit permit à la presse mexicaine de diffamer une fois de plus Tina Modotti. Mais paradoxalement, au moment où ses activités politiques occupaient tant de gens, le travail de photographe de Modotti était de plus en plus reconnu au niveau international. Des articles sur elle se succédaient dans des revues comme *Creative Art, transition* et *BIFUR*. Elle était même une caution publicitaire pour les films Agfa.

Au début de 1930, un attentat dirigé contre le président du Mexique et une vague de répression consécutive sur les membres du PCM eurent pour conséquence l'arrestation et l'extradition de Tina Modotti. Elle retrouva Vittorio Vidali, agent soviétique, italien comme elle, qu'elle avait rencontré à Mexico en 1927, et à qui la liaient des liens d'amitié qui se resserrèrent sur le bateau qui les conduisait en Europe. Il essaya de la convaincre de l'accompagner à Moscou, mais elle souhaitait s'installer à Berlin. Là, elle fut en contact avec le Bauhaus, école de photographie, d'art et d'architecture dont elle connaissait déjà le travail par des publications. Elle rencontra la photographe Lotte Jacobi, qui organisa une exposition des œuvres de Modotti, laquelle fut très bien reçue par

Hands resting on tool, 1927

new surroundings. She complained bitterly in her letters about the light, her camera, and the Germans. The few photographs she did make there reflect her mood and are a somewhat cruel parody of German life.

Within six months Modotti had given in to Vidali's persuasion and joined him in Moscow. Once there, she realized that her photography did not comply with socialist realism, Stalin's concept of "revolutionary" art. She decided to give up the camera completely, a decision she had been considering for some time, to devote herself to combating fascism through work for International Red Aid. Her choice of political activism over art is understandable in the context of the absolutist idealism of her time.

Using various identities, she entered fascist-controlled countries to assist the families of political prisoners. Detection would almost certainly have meant torture, and even death. In 1936, Modotti and Vidali were in Spain for the outbreak of the Civil War. He became renowned in the defense of

lung mit Arbeiten Modottis, die von den Kritikern positiv aufgenommen wurde. Modotti hatte jedoch große Schwierigkeiten, sich in ihrer neuen Umgebung einzugewöhnen. In ihren Briefen beklagte sie sich bitterlich über das Licht, ihre Kamera und die Deutschen. Die wenigen Aufnahmen, die sie in dieser Zeit machte, spiegeln diese Stimmung wider und sind eine bissige Parodie auf das Leben in Deutschland.

Innerhalb von sechs Monaten war Modotti soweit, Vidalis Überredungskünsten nachzugeben und ihm nach Moskau zu folgen. Dort angekommen erkannte sie, daß ihre Fotografie nicht dem von Stalin angeordneten Konzept »revolutionärer« Kunst, dem sozialistischen Realismus, entsprach. Sie beschloß, die Fotografie aufzugeben – eine Entscheidung, die sie schon länger erwogen hatte – und sich bei der Internationalen Roten Hilfe ganz dem Kampf gegen den Faschismus zu verschreiben. Ihr Entschluß, die Kunst der politischen Arbeit zu opfern, ist vor dem Hintergrund des damaligen absoluten Idealismus zu verstehen.

Unter verschiedenen Identitäten reiste Modotti in faschistisch regierte Staaten, um den Familien politischer Gefangener zu helfen. Ihre Enttarnung hätte dabei höchstwahrscheinlich Folter oder sogar den Tod bedeutet. 1936 befanden sich Modotti und Vidali bei Ausbruch des Bürgerkriegs in Spanien. Vidali er-

les critiques locales. Mais Modotti ne parvenait pas à s'adapter à son nouvel environnement. Elle se plaint amèrement dans ses lettres, de la lumière, de son appareil et des Allemands. Les quelques photos prises là-bas reflètent son humeur et sont une parodie quelque peu cruelle du mode de vie allemand.

En l'espace de six mois, elle se rendait aux arguments de Vidali et le rejoignait à Moscou. Une fois là-bas, elle réalisa que son travail ne correspondait pas aux exigences du « réalisme socialiste », la conception stalinienne de ce que devait être un art « révolutionnaire ». Elle décida alors de renoncer entièrement à la photo, comme elle y songeait depuis quelque temps, pour se consacrer à la lutte contre le fascisme en travaillant pour le Secours rouge international. C'est au regard de l'idéalisme absolu de son époque qu'il faut comprendre son choix de l'activisme politique au détriment de son art.

Utilisant plusieurs identités différentes, elle pénétra dans des pays sous régimes fascistes pour y assister les familles des prisonniers politiques. En cas d'arrestation, elle encourait presque certainement la torture et la mort. En 1936, Modotti et Vidali étaient en Espagne dès le début de la guerre civile. Il parti-

Madrid as "Comandante Carlos," and Modotti, under the name Maria, played a key role in directing international aid to the Republican cause. Following Franco's victory in 1939, she returned reluctantly to Mexico. Living incognito as Dr. Carmen Sanchez, she avoided her friends from the 1920s, associating mainly with fellow political refugees from fascism.

In 1940, Modotti worked with a photographic expedition for a book documenting President Lazaro Cardenas's revolution in health, education, and land reform in Mexico, but she refused to take any photographs. Towards the end of 1941, she began to contact some of her old friends, such as the muralist José Clemente Orozco, and there is an indication that she was trying to acquire a camera to start photographing again. But fate intervened, and on the night of January 6, 1942, on her way home from a dinner party given by her friend, Bauhaus architect Hannes Meyer, Modotti died of an alleged heart attack in the back seat of a Mexico City taxicab.

langte bei der Verteidigung Madrids als »Comandante Carlos« Berühmtheit, und Modotti spielte unter dem Decknamen Maria eine zentrale Rolle bei der Organisation der internationalen Hilfe für die republikanische Sache. Nach Francos Sieg 1939 kehrte sie widerwillig nach Mexiko zurück. Sie lebte dort inkognito unter dem Namen Dr. Carmen Sanchez, mied ihre Freunde aus den zwanziger Jahren und verkehrte hauptsächlich mit Menschen, die wie sie vor dem Faschismus geflüchtet waren.

1940 nahm Modotti an einer fotografischen Expedition für ein Buch über Präsident Lazaro Cardenas' Revolution im Gesundheits- und Bildungswesen und die von ihm eingeleitete Landreform in Mexiko teil. Allerdings lehnte sie es ab, selbst zu fotografieren. Gegen Ende des Jahres 1941 nahm sie, zu einigen ihrer alten Freunde, wie etwa dem Wandmaler José Clemente Orozco, wieder Kontakt auf. Es gibt außerdem Hinweise darauf, daß sie versucht hat, eine Kamera zu erwerben, um wieder mit dem Fotografieren anzufangen. Doch es sollte anders kommen: Als Modotti am 6. Januar 1942 in Mexico City nach einer Abendgesellschaft ihres Freundes, des Bauhaus-Architekten Hannes Meyer, in einem Taxi nach Hause fuhr, starb sie während der Fahrt auf dem Rücksitz des Wagens, angeblich an einem Herzanfall.

cipa à la défense de Madrid sous le titre de « Comandante Carlos » tandis qu'elle, sous le nom de Maria, jouait un rôle decisif dans l'organisation de l'aide internationale à la cause républicaine. Après la défaite des républicains en 1939, elle rentra à contrecœur au Mexique. Vivant sous une identité d'emprunt – Dr. Carmen Sanchez – elle évita ses amis des années 20, préférant la compagnie de réfugiés politiques en provenance de pays sous contrôle fasciste.

En 1940, Modotti participa à une expédition photographique pour un ouvrage sur les réformes conduites par le président Lazaro Cardenas dans les domaines de la santé, de l'éducation et de la réforme agraire au Mexique, mais elle refusa de prendre elle-même la moindre photo. Vers la fin de 1941, elle reprit peu à peu contact avec certains de ses anciens amis, comme le fresquiste José Clemente Orozco, et on dispose d'éléments permettant de penser qu'elle s'apprêtait à acheter un appareil pour recommencer à photographier. Mais le destin en décida autrement : dans la nuit du 6 janvier 1942, rentrant d'un dîner chez son ami, l'architecte du Bauhaus Hannes Meyer, Modotti mourut de ce qu'on présuma être une crise cardiaque sur le siège arrière d'un taxi de Mexico.

Hands of the puppeteer, 1929

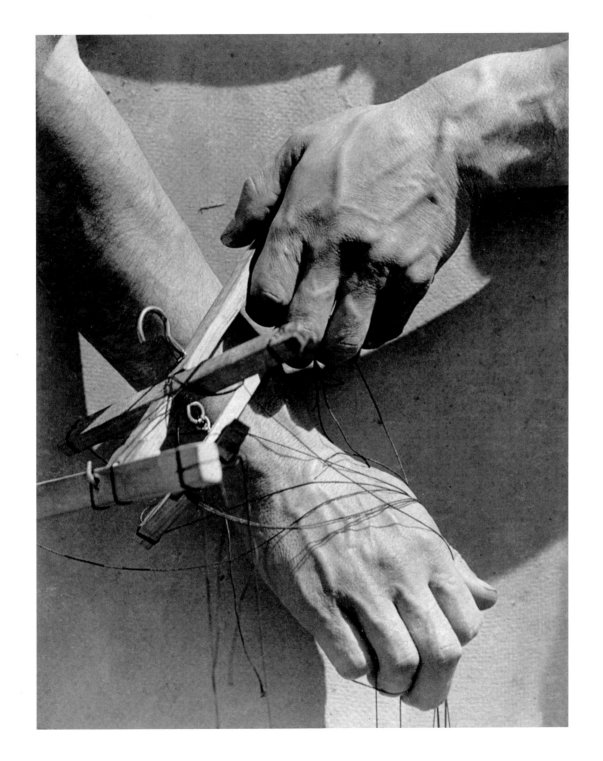

Louis Bunin with dancing puppet, 1929

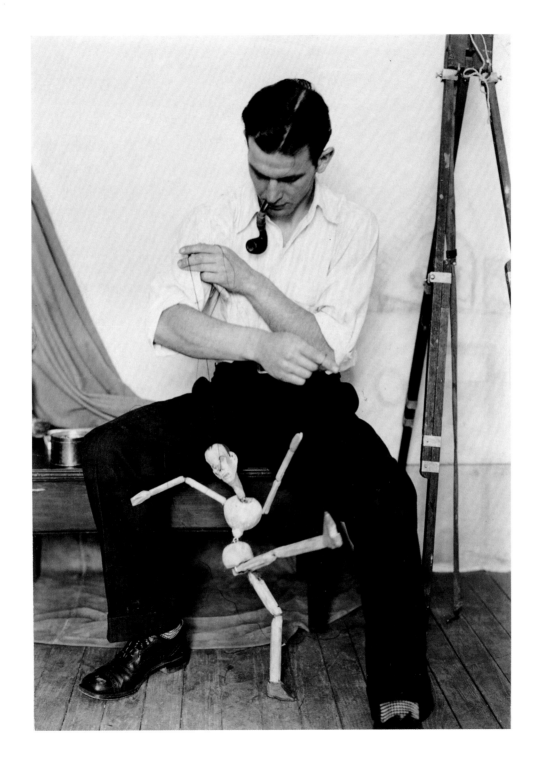

31

Police puppets, 1929

Women of Tehuantepec, 1929

Pacheco painting a mural, 1927

José Clemente Orozco at work, 1927

Circus tent, 1924

Scaffolding, ca. 1925

Telephone wires, 1925

Tank no. 1, 1927

Interior of church, Tepotzotlan, 1924

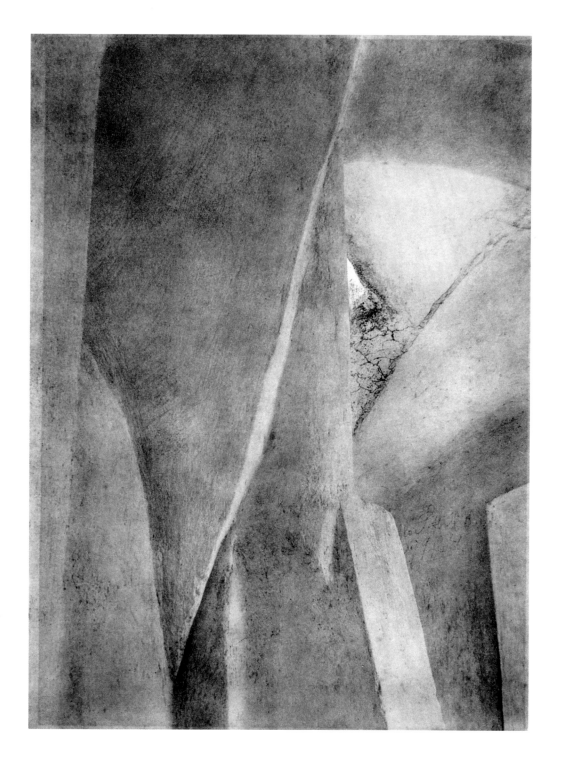

49

Stadium, Mexico City, ca. 1927

Julio Antonio Mella's typewriter, 1928

Mexican sombrero with hammer and sickle, 1927

Bandolier, corn, guitar, 1927

Wine glasses, 1925

Mexican peasants reading El Machete, 1928

Workers' parade, 1926

Antonieta Rivas Mercado, 1929

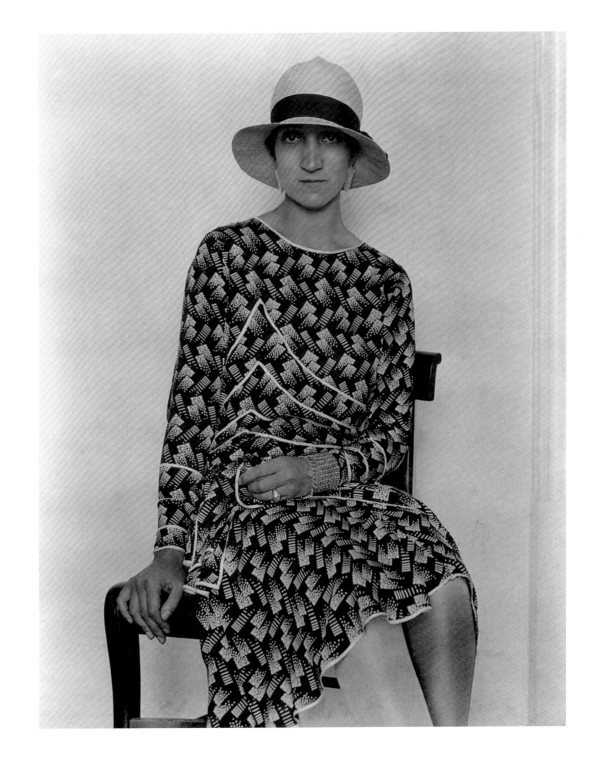

Three ways to wear a serape, ca. 1927

German youth group, 1930

Loading bananas, Veracruz, 1928

Luz Jimenez breast-feeding her baby, ca. 1925

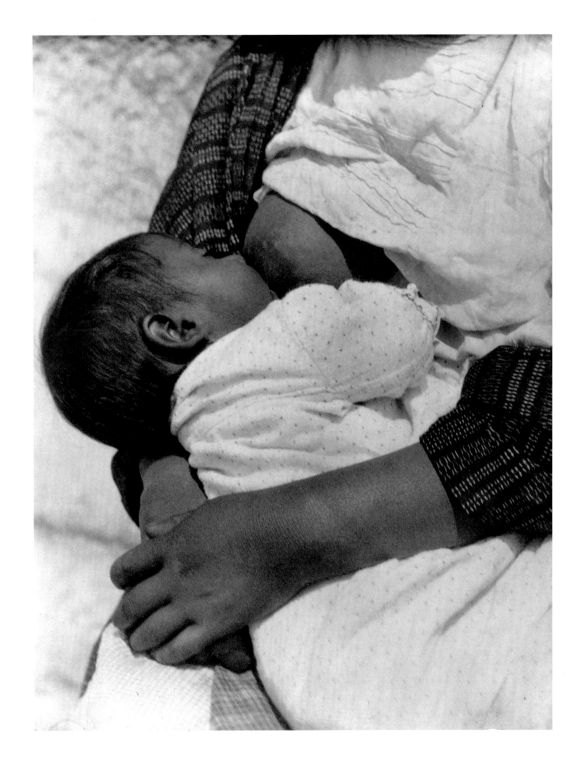

Workers, ca. 1926–29

Poverty and elegance, 1928

Rafael on the "azotea", ca. 1924

A peasant family in Veracruz, 1927

Fiesta in Juchitán, 1929

Vittorio Vidali, 1930

Diego Rivera and Frida Kahlo at the May Day march, 1929

Detail of *In the Arsenal,* Diego Rivera mural at the Ministry of Education, Mexico City, 1928

Julio Antonio Mella, 1928

CHRONOLOGY	CHRONOLOGIE	CHRONOLOGIE

CHRONOLOGY

1896 Born August 17, Udine, Italy.
1898 Moves with family to Austria.
1905 Returns to Udine.
1908 Begins working in silk factory.

1913 Emigrates to the United States, joining father and sister in San Francisco.
1915 Attends Pan-Pacific Exposition and meets future husband, poet and painter Roubaix de l'Abrie Richey (Robo).

17–18 Performs in local Italian theater. Moves to Los Angeles.
1920 Acts in silent films. Plays leading role in *The Tiger's Coat*.
1921 Begins posing for Edward Weston.
1922 Trip to Mexico where Robo dies suddenly. Arranges exhibit of work by Robo, Weston, and other California artists.

1923 Moves to Mexico with Weston, manages his studio, and begins taking photographs with Korona camera.
1924 First exhibit of work, wins runner-up prize. Begins collaboration with *Mexican Folkways* magazine.
1925 Becomes official photographer of Diego Rivera's murals, temporarily takes over Weston's studio work, and shows with him in joint exhibit.
1926 Starts using Graflex camera. Wins prize in collective exhibit. Travels throughout Mexico with Edward and Brett Weston taking photographs to illustrate Anita Brenner's *Idols Behind Altars*. Becomes involved in proposed film on history of Mexican revolution using her photographs of murals. Weston leaves Mexico.

CHRONOLOGIE

Geboren am 17. August in Udine, Italien.
Umzug der Familie nach Österreich.
Rückkehr nach Udine.
Beginnt, in einer Seidenfabrik zu arbeiten.

Emigration in die Vereinigten Staaten, zu Vater und Schwester nach San Francisco.
Besuch der Pan-Pacific Exposition und erste Begegnung mit ihrem späteren Ehemann, dem Dichter und Maler Roubaix de l'Abrie Richey (Robo).

Auftritte im örtlichen italienischen Theater. Umzug nach Los Angeles.
Schauspielerin in Stummfilmen. Hauptrolle in *The Tiger's Coat*.
Arbeitet als Modell für Edward Weston.
Reise nach Mexiko, wo Robo unerwartet stirbt. Organisation einer Ausstellung mit Werken von Robo, Weston und anderen kalifornischen Künstlern.

Umzug nach Mexiko mit Weston, Mitarbeit in seinem Atelier und erste fotografische Arbeiten mit einer Korona-Kamera.
Erste Teilnahme an Ausstellung, erhält Auszeichnung. Beginn der Zusammenarbeit mit der Zeitschrift *Mexican Folkways*.
Wird offizielle Fotografin von Riveras Wandbildern, übernimmt vorübergehend Westons Atelierarbeit und stellt mit ihm aus.
Beginnt, mit einer Graflex-Kamera zu arbeiten. Auszeichnung bei einer Gemeinschaftsausstellung. Mexikoreise mit Edward und Brett Weston für Aufnahmen zur Illustration von Anita Brenners *Idols Behind Altars*. Beteiligung an einem Filmvorhaben über die Geschichte der mexikanischen Revolution, in dem ihre Aufnahmen von Wandbildern Verwendung finden. Weston verläßt Mexiko.

CHRONOLOGIE

Née le 17 août à Udine, Italie.
La famille s'installe en Autriche.
Retour à Udine.
Commence à travailler dans une usine de soie.

Emigre aux Etats-Unis, rejoignant son père et sa sœur à San Francisco.
Visite l'exposition Pan-pacifique où elle rencontre son futur mari, le poète et peintre Roubaix de l'Abrie Richey (dit Robo).

Se produit dans le théâtre italien local. S'installe à Los Angeles.
Joue dans des films muets. Rôle principal dans *The Tiger's Coat*.
Commence à poser pour Edward Weston.
Voyage au Mexique ; mort soudaine de Robo. Organisation d'une exposition des œuvres de Robo, Weston et d'autres artistes californiens.
S'installe à Mexico avec Weston, dirige son studio et commence à prendre des photos avec un appareil Korona.
Première exposition de son travail, gagne un prix. Début d'une collaboration avec le magazine *Mexican Folkways*.
Photographe officielle des fresques de Diego Rivera, ce qui prend temporairement le dessus sur son travail au studio de Weston. Exposition conjointe avec Weston.
Commence à utiliser un appareil Graflex. Remporte un prix dans une exposition collective. Voyage à travers le Mexique avec Edward et Brett Weston, prenant des photos pour illustrer *Idols Behind Altars* d'Anita Brenner. S'engage dans un projet proposé de film sur l'histoire de la révolution mexicaine utilisant ses photos de fresques. Weston quitte le Mexique.

Edward Weston, 1924

1927 Joins Mexican Communist Party. Takes photographs of Party events and to illustrate *El Canto de Los Hombres* by *estridenista* poet German List Arzubide. Publishes work in *New Masses* and *Creative Art.*

1928 Lives with Cuban rebel, Julio Antonio Mella. Embarks on photojournalism project for party newspaper, *El Machete.* Shares first prize in collective show. Continues publishing in *AIZ, New Masses,* and *Creative Art.*

1929 Mella gunned down by her side. Ensuing murder trial attacks Modotti's morality. Visits Tehuantepec and photographs local women. Agfa uses work to endorse their film. Publishes in *Vanity Fair.* First solo exhibit.

1930 Framed for attack on Mexican president, arrested and expelled from Mexico. Travels to Berlin. Experiences difficulty in continuing her photography. Moves to Moscow. Joins Soviet Communist Party and becomes immersed in political work.

1931 Gives up photography. Works full time for Comintern.

1932–33 Based in Paris, carries out undercover missions throughout Europe to aid political prisoners and their families.

1935–39 Participates in Spanish Civil War as "Maria," working for International Red Aid.

1939 Returns to Mexico incognito.

1942 Dies in Mexico City taxicab in the early hours of January 6.

Beitritt zur Kommunistischen Partei Mexikos. Aufnahmen von Parteiveranstaltungen und Illustration von *El Canto de Los Hombres* des *estridenista*-Dichters German List Arzubide. Veröffentlichungen ihrer Arbeiten in *New Masses* und *Creative Art.*

Lebt mit dem kubanischen Revolutionär Julio Antonio Mella. Beginn eines fotojournalistischen Projekts für die Parteizeitung *El Machete.* Beteiligung am ersten Preis in einer Gemeinschaftsausstellung. Weitere Veröffentlichungen in *AIZ, New Masses* und *Creative Art.*

Mella wird an ihrer Seite erschossen. Im anschließenden Mordprozeß wird Modottis Lebensstil als unmoralisch angeprangert. Reise nach Tehuantepec und Aufnahmen der dort lebenden Frauen. Agfa wirbt mit ihren Arbeiten für seine Filme. Veröffentlichungen in *Vanity Fair.* Erste Einzelausstellung.

Nach einem Attentat auf den mexikanischen Präsidenten folgen Verhaftung und Ausweisung aus Mexiko. Aufenthalt in Berlin. Schwierigkeiten mit ihrer fotografischen Arbeit. Umzug nach Moskau. Beitritt zur dortigen Kommunistischen Partei und Konzentration auf die politische Arbeit.

Aufgabe ihrer fotografischen Arbeit. Widmet ihre ganze Kraft der Komintern.

Führt von Paris aus geheime Hilfsaktionen für politische Gefangene und ihre Familien in ganz Europa durch.

Teilnahme am Spanischen Bürgerkrieg unter dem Decknamen »Maria« im Auftrag der Internationalen Roten Hilfe.

Rückkehr nach Mexiko unter anderem Namen.

Stirbt in den frühen Morgenstunden des 6. Januar in einem Taxi in Mexico City.

Entre au Parti communiste mexicain. Photographie des manifestations du Parti et illustre *El Canto de Los Hombres* du poète de l'*estridenista* German List Arzubide. Publie dans *New Masses* et dans *Creative Art.*

Vit avec un exilé cubain, Julio Antonio Mella. Se lance dans un projet de photojournalisme pour le journal du Parti, *El Machete.* Partage un premier prix dans une exposition collective. Continue à publier dans *AIZ, New Masses* et *Creative Art.*

Mella est abattu à côté d'elle. Lors du procès du meurtre, Modotti est attaquée sur sa moralité. Voyage à Tehuantepec et photographie des femmes autochtones. Agfa utilise ses travaux pour la promotion de ses films. Publie dans *Vanity Fair.* Première exposition en solo.

Faussement accusée d'un attentat contre le président du Mexique, elle est arrêtée et extradée. Voyage à Berlin. Eprouve des difficultés à continuer la photographie. S'installe à Moscou, où elle entre au Parti communiste soviétique et s'immerge dans l'activisme politique.

Abandonne la photo. Travaille à temps plein pour le Komintern.

Basée à Paris, elle remplit des missions clandestines d'aide aux prisonniers politiques et à leurs familles dans toute l'Europe.

Participe à la guerre civile espagnole sous le nom de « Maria », en travaillant pour le Secours rouge international.

Rentre au Mexique incognito.

Décède dans un taxi à Mexico aux premières heures du 6 janvier.

SELECTED BIBLIOGRAPHY
AUSWAHLBIBLIOGRAPHIE
BIBLIOGRAPHIE SÉLECTIVE

BOOKS AND CATALOGS
BÜCHER UND KATALOGE
LIVRES ET CATALOGUES

Barckhausen Canale, Cristianne. *Verdad y Leyenda de Tina Modotti*. Havana: Casa de las Americas, 1989.

Constantine, Mildred. *A Fragile Life*. New York: Rizzoli, 1983.

Hooks, Margaret. *Tina Modotti: Photographer & Revolutionary*. London: Pandora/Harper Collins, 1993.

Modotti, Tina, ed. *The Book of Robo*. Los Angeles: n.p., 1923.

Modotti, Tina. *The Letters from Tina Modotti to Edward Weston. The Archive*. Tucson: Center for Creative Photography, University of Arizona. 1986. No. 22.

Newhall, Nancy, ed. *The Daybooks of Edward Weston: I. Mexico*. Millerton, New York: Aperture, 1973.

Philadelphia Museum of Art. *Tina Modotti Photographs*. New York: Harry N. Abrams Inc., 1996.

Vidali, Vittorio. *Retrato de mujer*. Puebla: Universidad Autonoma de Puebla, 1984.

Whitechapel Art Gallery. *Frida Kahlo and Tina Modotti*. London: Whitechapel Art Gallery, 1982.

ARTICLES/ARTIKEL

Beals, Carleton. "Tina Modotti." *Creative Arts*, February 1929. Vol. 4, no. 2.

Hooks, Margaret. "Assignment, Mexico: Mystery of the Missing Modottis." *Afterimage*, November 1991. Vol. 19, no. 4.

Kramer, Hilton. "Tina Modotti's Brief but Remarkable Career." *New York Times*, January 23, 1977.

Modotti, Tina. "On Photography." *Mexican Folkways*, October–December 1929. Vol. 5, no. 4.

Rivera, Diego. "Edward Weston and Tina Modotti." *Mexican Folkways*, April–May 1926. Vol. 20, no. 1.

Vestal, David. "Tina's Trajectory." *Infinity*, 1966. Vol. 15, no. 2.

PUBLICATIONS IN WHICH MODOTTI PUBLISHED HER WORK
PUBLIKATIONEN MIT BEITRÄGEN VON MODOTTI
PUBLICATIONS COMPORTANT DES TRAVAUX DE TINA MODOTTI

Books/Bücher/Livres
Brenner, Anita. *Idols Behind Altars*. New York: Biblo & Tannen, 1929.

Das Riveras. Berlin: n.p., 1928.

Evans, Ernestine. *The Frescos of Diego Rivera*. New York: Delphic Studios, 1932.

Reed, Alma. *José Clemente Orozco*. New York: Delphic Studios, 1932.

Smith, Susan. *Made in Mexico*. New York: Knopf, 1930.

Periodicals/Zeitschriften/Périodiques
Arbeiter Illustrierte Zeitung (*AIZ*). Berlin, 1928–31.

BIFUR. Paris, 1928.

Contemporaneos. Mexico City, 1927–30.

Creative Art. New York and London, 1929.

CROM Magazine. Mexico City, 1927–30.

Forma. Mexico City, 1926–28.

Horizonte. Jalapa, Mexico, 1926–28.

International Literature. Moscow, 1935–36.

L'Art Vivant. Paris, 1930.

El Machete. Mexico City, 1926–29.

Mexican Life. Mexico City, 1925–31.

Mexican Folkways. Mexico City, 1924–30.

New Masses. New York, 1927–30.

Revista de revistas. Mexico City, 1930–42 and 1917–18.

transition. Paris, 1929.

El Universal Grafico. Mexico City, 1929–30.

El Universal Ilustrado. Mexico City, 1922–30.

SOLO EXHIBITIONS
EINZELAUSSTELLUNGEN
EXPOSITIONS PERSONNELLES

1929 Biblioteca Nacional, Mexico City.
1930 Studio of Lotte Jacobi, Berlin.
1942 Galeria de Arte Mexicano, Mexico City.
1977 Museum of Modern Art, New York.
1995 Philadelphia Museum of Art, Philadelphia.

OTHER EXHIBITIONS
ANDERE AUSSTELLUNGEN
AUTRES EXPOSITIONS

1924 Palacio de Mineria, Mexico City.
1925 State Museum of Guadalajara, Jalisco, Mexico.
1926 Galeria de Arte Moderno, Mexico City.
1927 *Tenth International Salon of Photography*. Los Angeles Museum, California.
1929 Berkeley Art Museum, California.
1930 Harvard Society for Contemporary Art, Cambridge, Massachusetts.
1932 Brooklyn Museum, New York.
1982 Whitechapel Gallery, London.

APERTURE MASTERS OF PHOTOGRAPHY